JONAS
SALK

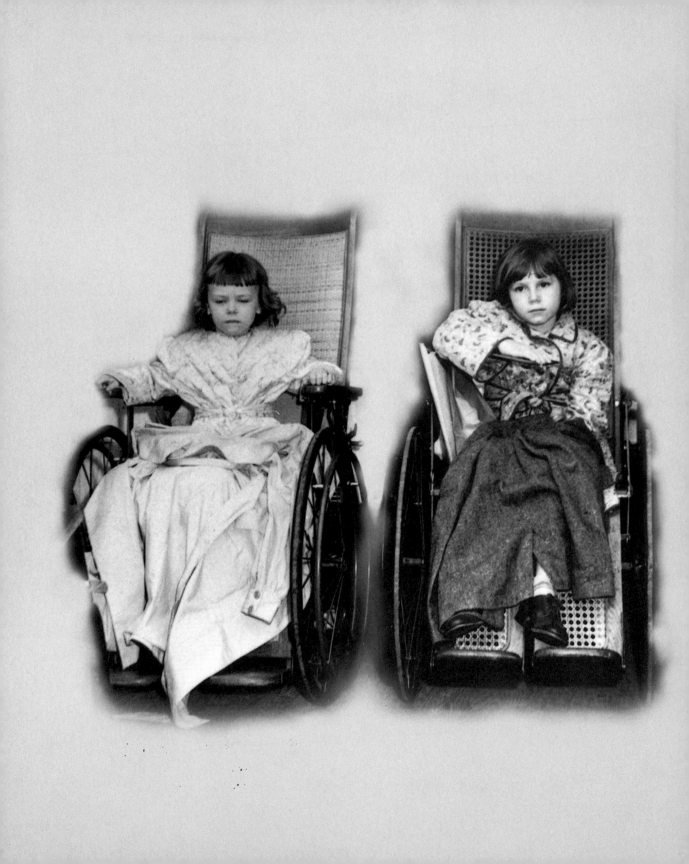

JONAS SALK

Polio Pioneer

**Corinne J. Naden
and Rose Blue**

A Gateway Biography
THE MILLBROOK PRESS
Brookfield, Connecticut

ACKNOWLEDGMENTS
The authors thank Dr. Harrison Wein, Office of the Director, National Institutes of Health, Bethesda, Maryland; and Dr. William Nathan, Executive Faculty, Menninger Clinic, Topeka, Kansas, for their scientific input and helpful suggestions. We also thank Helen Harris, New York City Board of Education, for her assistance as reading consultant.

Cover photographs courtesy of Liaison Agency/Hulton Getty; Liaison Agency/Eric Lawton; UPI Corbis-Bettmann

Photographs courtesy of UPI/Corbis-Bettmann: pp. 2, 11 (bottom), 21 (top), 36; Liaison Agency/Hulton Getty: pp. 6, 35; Archive Photos: pp. 9, 30, 41 (© Reuters/Kamal Kishore); March of Dimes Birth Defect Foundation: pp. 11 (top), 32 (both), 34; Corbis-Bettmann: pp. 15, 18, 21 (bottom), 26 (both), ; Franklin D. Roosevelt Library: p. 22 (both); Liaison Agency: p. 39 (© Eric Lawton); Corbis: p. 43 (© Bradley Smith)

Library of Congress Cataloging-in-Publication Data
Naden, Corinne J.
    Jonas Salk : polio pioneer / Corinne J. Naden and Rose Blue.
        p. cm. – (A Gateway biography)
    Includes index.
    ISBN 0-7613-1804-6 (lib. bdg.)
       1. Salk, Jonas, 1914——Juvenile literature. 2. Virologists—United
    States—Biography—Juvenile literature. 3. Poliomyelitis vaccine—Juvenile literature.
    [1. Salk, Jonas, 1914- 2. Scientists. 3. Poliomyelitis vaccine.] I. Blue, Rose. II. Title. III.
    Series.
    QR31.S25 N334 2001
    610'.92—dc21   [B] 00-048023

Published by The Millbrook Press, Inc.
2 Old New Milford Road
Brookfield, Connecticut 06804
www.millbrookpress.com

JONAS SALK

Many children who had polio could not walk without leg braces.

*I*magine a killer so small that you cannot see it. You can't touch it, and you can't hear it. But you know it's there. A frightening thought, isn't it? Lots of people had those frightening thoughts back in the 1940s and 1950s. What were they afraid of? The killer's name is polio, or poliomyelitis. It comes from two Greek words, *polio*, which means "gray," and *myelos*, which means "spinal cord." So, the name means a disease of the gray matter, which is part of the nerve tissue inside the spine. It is a silent disease, invisible and deadly.

Polio is a disease that often paralyzes arms and legs and even chest muscles. Polio used to be called "infantile paralysis" because it struck so many children. Many of them could never walk again, not without crutches or leg braces. Some could not breathe without the help of machines. One of those machines was called an iron lung. This long, round tube made of stainless steel encloses a patient from the neck down. The iron lung breathes for someone whose chest muscles don't work.

Polio struck terror all over the world. Nobody knew where it came from, whom it would strike, or how to stop it. Yet, for most young people today, polio is a disease that doesn't exist. Why? Because of a real-life American hero named Dr. Jonas Salk. Convinced he was right even when others disagreed, Jonas Salk developed a vaccine that freed the world from polio and the great fear that surrounded it. This is his story.

*I*t was 1916 and another long, hot summer in New York City. But this one was different. A polio epidemic had hit the United States. Epidemics always seemed to happen in the summer, so health officials thought it must have been due to the crowds of people. There were crowds in theaters and swimming pools, so health officials closed those places and told parents to keep their children away from almost everybody.

A machine called an iron lung helped polio victims breathe when their chest muscles were not working.

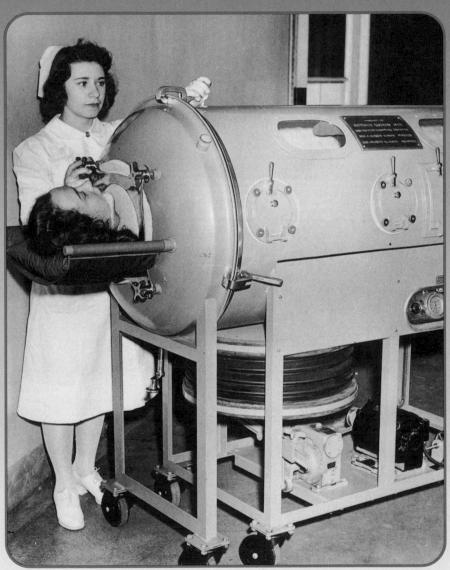

Like lots of other New Yorkers, Daniel and Dora Salk were worried. Their son Jonas, born in New York City on October 28, 1914, was nearly two years old. What is this terrible disease, they asked.

Polio is a disease caused by a virus, which is a tiny germ. Viruses cause lots of illnesses, such as measles and the common cold. But the poliovirus is scary because it affects nerves in the spinal cord.

Nerves in the human body carry signals from the brain, through the spinal cord to different parts of the body, telling the muscles what to do. For instance, your brain sends a message through your nerves to your arm. The message says "move your arm," and so you move your arm. But the poliovirus attacks those nerves. Then, if your brain says "move your arm," your nerves can't send the message to your muscles, and you can't move your arm.

Young Jonas didn't get polio during the epidemic in 1916. His family soon moved from Manhattan to the Bronx, the northernmost borough of New York City. He went to grade school there. He was an excellent student. When it was time for high school, he was not only smart but also lucky. The City College of New York (CCNY)—now known as the City University of New York (CUNY)—was sponsoring special schools. The schools took only gifted

Public places, such as pools, closed when polio became an epidemic.

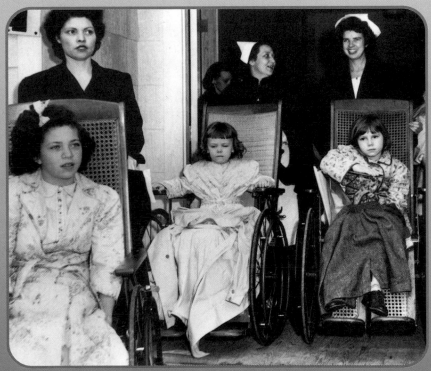

The poliovirus paralyzed many young people, who were left in wheelchairs during their childhood. Some of the more severe cases were paralyzed permanently.

students who could finish four years of high school in three years.

Twelve-year-old Jonas Salk passed the test and entered Townsend Harris High School in 1926. When he graduated three years later, he was not quite fifteen and was ready for college. But who would pay for it? The Salks by now had two other sons to raise. CCNY came to the rescue once again. It offered free schooling to some New York City students. Salk was one of them.

He entered college in 1929 with his eye on law school. But by the time he graduated in 1934, he changed his mind and decided to become a doctor, which pleased his parents. They thought he might open up a nice little office in the city.

That's not quite how it worked out. First there was medical school at the New York University College of Medicine. After his first year of medical school, Jonas Salk spent one year working in a laboratory and then returned to his medical studies. He graduated on June 8, 1939, and the next day married Donna Lindsay, whom he had met in 1937.

Right after graduation, Jonas Salk worked for a few months in the laboratory of Dr. Thomas Francis Jr., a professor at NYU Medical School. Dr. Francis was highly respected in the field of microbiology.

Microbiology is the study of tiny forms of life called microbes (bacteria and viruses). Dr. Francis was looking into the possibility of making a vaccine from a killed virus.

Let's suppose a mouse gets a virus that carries influenza, or the flu. The mouse gets the flu because it now has the live influenza virus in its body. Francis thought that, in the lab, he could remove the live flu virus from the mouse's lungs. Then he could kill the live flu virus with a special ray. Next, he could make the killed virus into a vaccine. If the vaccine were injected into a person, he or she would probably not get the flu. Why? The answer is antibodies.

Let's say you are injected with the killed flu virus. That killed virus makes your body produce proteins called antibodies. Then a flu virus enters your body. Your body recognizes that the flu virus is something that shouldn't be there. The antibodies rush out to fight it. And you don't get the flu.

It may sound easy, but fighting a virus with a vaccine is tricky work. The vaccine must be strong enough so your body will make antibodies. But it can't be so strong that you get sick from the vaccine!

All vaccines work in the same way, whether for flu, measles, or polio. Antibodies fight invaders such as germs that want to enter your body and make you sick. The army of fighters against invaders is known as the immune system. A healthy immune system can fight off lots of germs and keep you well. Your immune system also has a memory. It remembers, for instance, that you have had a flu shot. So, if the flu virus comes along, out rush your antibodies to fight off the flu.

In March 1940, Jonas Salk left the laboratory for two years so he could intern. This is when new doctors work in a hospital with more experienced medical people. They learn hospital routines and how to deal with patients. One of the country's best places to intern was Mount Sinai Hospital in New York City. Out of the 250 new doctors who applied that year, only 12 were chosen for an internship at Mount Sinai. Dr. Salk was one of them.

In 1942, the internship was over and Salk was looking for a job. He wrote a letter to his old teacher, Dr. Francis, who was now at the University of Michigan in Ann Arbor. Did Francis have a job for him?

In the meantime, the U.S. government also had a job for Dr. Salk. Since 1941, the United States had been fighting World War II. Salk received a message from his draft board that he could either join the military or get a job researching something important to national defense.

Dr. Jonas Salk was chosen to do an internship at Mount Sinai Hospital in New York City.

Salk decided to work for Dr. Francis at the School of Public Health. Francis was working on a vaccine against the flu, and the U.S. Army wanted the vaccine quickly. So Francis and Salk concentrated on finding a workable flu vaccine. And they did. Salk proved in the lab that the flu virus could be killed by a solution called formalin. A vaccine made from this killed virus could be injected into the body to start making antibodies to fight off the disease.

By the winter of 1943, Francis and Salk had produced a flu vaccine in the lab. But would it work on people? Like all lab experiments, the vaccine had to be tested "in the field." The flu vaccine was tested on about two thousand soldiers in a double-blind test: Half were given the vaccine, and the other half were injected with a harmless liquid called a placebo, which contains no medicine. No soldier knew which injection he got. The results showed that the vaccinated men had 75 percent fewer cases of the flu. It worked.

World War II ended in 1945. Although he was pleased with his work in Michigan, Salk was restless. Jonas Salk was a brilliant man, but he was a difficult man, too. Ambitious and driven, he was convinced that his way was the right way.

Many of his colleagues thought him too ambitious and too confident, criticisms that followed Salk all his life. He seemed not to notice. In fact, he once said, "Life is not a popularity contest. I learned that a long time ago. I'm not running for office or a position . . . and I've been able to do the things that I felt moved to do." At age thirty-three, Salk decided that he wanted his own lab so he could do his own research in his own way. In addition, he had a family to think about. The Salks now had two sons, Peter and Darrell, and later had a third, Jonathan.

Salk decided that he especially wanted to study the body's immune system. Why do some people get sick and others don't, even when they are all exposed to the same virus? The reason is the body's defense against disease, the immune system. Immunology is the study of that defense. That's where Jonas Salk wanted to spend his future.

Many scientists had contributed to the understanding of microorganisms (MI-kro-OR-gan-iz-ems), living things too small to be seen. A Dutchman, Antonie van Leeuwenhoek, made microscopes. In the 1670s, looking through one of his microscopes, he was able to see tiny, fuzzy, crawly things, or bacteria, in a drop of water.

Englishman Edward Jenner developed a vaccine against the fatal illness known as smallpox in the late 1790s. Hungarian doctor Ignaz Philipp Semmelweis came up with a new idea in the 1840s. He wanted to stop the high death rate in maternity wards, so he told the nurses and doctors to wash their hands! Nobody had realized that washing hands could stop the spread of germs from one person to another. Most of the hospital staff thought

Jonas Salk with his wife, Donna, and their sons, Jonathan,
Darrell, and Peter (left to right)

Semmelweis was crazy. But they washed their hands and the death rate dropped.

Research continued and scientists learned a lot about bacteria, the kind of germ that can be seen with a regular microscope. But for some diseases, no bacteria could be seen. Scientists decided that something they couldn't see caused these diseases. It wasn't until 1898 that someone gave a name to that something. Dutch scientist Martinus Beijerinck was studying a disease of tobacco plants. He was looking for germs. He couldn't see them, but he knew they were there. He gave these germs the somewhat disgusting-sounding name of "poisonous slime." In Latin, that translates as virus.

It took centuries to name a virus. It would take another thirty years to see one. Then, a new kind of microscope was invented. And there they were, just as they'd always been, tiny organisms, some looking like tennis balls when magnified tens of thousands of times under the microscope. This was the virus.

With research on his mind, Jonas Salk left Michigan for the University of Pittsburgh in Pennsylvania. He was going to continue his flu studies. Then came an offer from the National Foundation for Infantile Paralysis to take part in a special research program.

Since 1938, the foundation had been involved in the treatment and rehabilitation of polio victims. Jonas Salk and the National Foundation would become very important to each other.

Scientists had been battling polio for a long, long time. It was mostly a losing fight. In 1948, the country was suffering through another long polio epidemic. Before it ended, some 27,000 people had polio, some of whom died and many of whom were disabled in some way.

Hospitals filled. Parents kept their children out of swimming pools and movie theaters and away from crowds. No one could see it and nothing seemed to stop it. Penicillin and other antibiotics (medicines) were in use in the 1940s, but they were useless against polio. Antibiotics kill bacteria, but they don't kill a virus.

Jonas Salk's work was mostly supported by the National Foundation for Infantile Paralysis. During the 1940s, the foundation looked for all kinds of ways to raise money for polio research. President Franklin Delano Roosevelt was very involved in these efforts.

Roosevelt, known as FDR, came down with polio when he was thirty-nine years old. He survived the fever, but he could never again stand or walk without

Polio scared everyone. Here, six-year-old twin sisters and their parents protest a school order that stated the girl with polio is not permitted to attend school. The quote on the sign refers to the family doctor's statement about fighting the school order.

During the epidemic, famous people visited young polio patients in hospitals to cheer them up. Here, Babe Ruth, one of baseball's greatest stars, brings the patients gifts and ice cream.

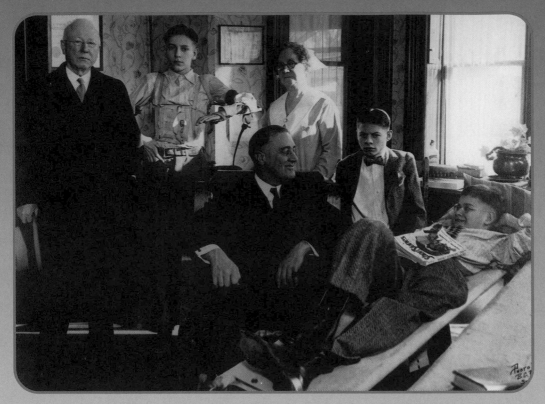

President Franklin Delano Roosevelt visits a polio patient in New York.

Roosevelt constantly encouraged people to contribute to the fight against polio.

the help of crutches or braces on his legs. Yet, he made light of it. In fact, after he became president in 1932, many Americans, even though they saw him in photographs, never realized that he had a physical disability.

Roosevelt worked hard for polio research while he was president. When he first got polio, he spent a lot of time in the soothing waters of a resort in Warm Springs, Georgia. The president later turned the resort into a therapy center for people with polio. But he had a problem raising money for it.

In those days, people tried to hide disabilities. Today, we are more open. People see athletes playing wheelchair basketball or competing in races such as the New York City Marathon. We know that wheelchairs or crutches don't have to stop a person's dreams from coming true.

Roosevelt thought that getting famous people to help would be a good money raiser. So, he asked a popular comedian named Eddie Cantor to get in touch with wealthy people and convince them to contribute money to fight polio. But Cantor said no. He had a better idea. Start a nationwide drive. Get everybody to contribute! Truckloads of money, mostly small amounts, began to pour in. Cantor called it the "march of dimes." Nearly three million dollars was sent to the White House!

The National Foundation for Infantile Paralysis changed its name to the National Foundation—March of Dimes in 1967. It changed again in 1979 and is now known as the March of Dimes Birth Defects Foundation. With polio all but gone today, it is dedicated to erasing birth defects and promoting health in all children.

In the late 1940s, the National Foundation's director of research, Harry M. Weaver, asked Salk to be part of a three-year study to find out how many different types of polio existed. That was important to know. If there was more than one type, then more than one vaccine probably would be needed.

Salk now began the project that would put him in the medical profession's hall of fame. The work was difficult, costly, and time consuming. At the time, testing methods involved the use of monkeys in the lab, and at most, one monkey could be used to test about three different viruses.

Then came a big discovery, but not from Salk's Pittsburgh lab. Help came from Boston, where in 1948 Dr. John Enders and his colleagues were studying the chicken pox virus. After one experiment, they had human embryo tissue left over, so they put some poliovirus in the test tubes.

They were amazed when the virus began to grow! Until then, scientists thought the virus could not grow outside of the body. But now that it could be made in tubes, scientists could grow the virus for research. Enders and his colleagues won the Nobel Prize for their work in 1954.

Salk saw Enders's discovery as a way to speed up his own project and find a path to a vaccine. By the end of the decade, Salk's lab research determined that among samples of poliovirus from more than one hundred patients in the United States, the varieties of poliovirus fell into one of three types. Therefore, a vaccine had to protect against all three. What a huge task!

In the lab, using monkey kidney tissue, Salk grew samples of the three kinds of poliovirus. He killed the virus with a chemical called formaldehyde. Salk believed that the virus that was killed and could not grow in the body would make a vaccine. He was afraid that a live virus in a vaccine could bring on the disease instead of preventing it. When he tested his killed vaccine on monkeys, none of them got polio.

Jonas Salk (left) with Dr. John Enders, who was one of three American polio specialists that won the 1954 Nobel Prize for Medicine.

Dr. Albert Sabin in his laboratory at the University of Cincinnati College of Medicine

The world of scientific research is small, and Salk's experiments were no secret. But instead of supporting him, many scientists were angry at Salk's work. Some just disliked his personality, which they considered conceited and distant. Some were jealous of the attention Salk received. They said he never gave credit to all the people who had worked on these problems before him. That complaint always followed Salk.

Mostly, he ignored others in his field. He was very uncomfortable with the fuss that swirled around him after his success. It is said he even tried to stop people from using the term "Salk vaccine."

Some scientists did not agree with Salk because they did not believe in a killed virus vaccine. The loudest disagreement was from Dr. Albert Bruce Sabin, leader of the live virus vaccine camp. There was more than professional jealousy here. It was a case of real disagreement between two people who felt strongly about their studies.

The rivalry between these two important medical people became bitter and lifelong. Sabin, who came to the United States from Poland in 1921, also graduated from New York University. He thought that a live poliovirus vaccine would be most effective.

But Salk ignored those who disagreed with him. He simply believed he was right. By mid-1952, he had performed enough lab tests to decide that his vaccine worked in monkeys. Now it was time to test it on people, which is always the difficult part of any untried medicine. It all means nothing if people can't take it.

Salk first tested his vaccine on humans in June 1952. There were forty-five disabled boys and girls who had previously recovered from polio, and twenty-seven staff members at the D.T. Watson Home for Crippled Children near Pittsburgh. Nobody got sick, but it was a scary time. Salk later said, "When you inoculate children with a polio vaccine, you don't sleep well for two or three weeks."

Later on in the testing, Salk injected himself and his family, including his third son Jonathan, then three years old. By early 1953, more than five hundred volunteers, both adults and children, had received the vaccine safely and had developed antibodies.

With this success, the National Foundation wanted to make an announcement. Salk was very careful and wanted to do more tests. But people were finding out the secret. A newspaper article printed a story on a "new polio vaccine." Rumor said that the respected *Journal of the American Medical Association* (JAMA) was reporting the success in its March issue.

Salk was worried that people were expecting too much. So, on March 26, 1953, Salk spoke to the country over the radio. Most people had never heard of him or his vaccine. But they had heard of polio, so they listened. The doctor explained what caused polio, what the virus was, and how the experimental vaccine worked. He also explained that a vaccine that could be used widely would not be ready for some time.

Late in 1953, Basil O'Conner of the National Foundation announced that the vaccine would go into field trials the following year. This meant testing on a large number of children who never had polio. It was to be the largest field trial of a vaccine ever. It was organized by Salk's teacher, Dr. Thomas Francis at the University of Michigan. The field trials would include double-blind tests: Half would get the real vaccine and half would get a fake vaccine. Nobody but Dr. Francis knew who got the real one and who got the fake one. Not even Salk would know the results until Dr. Francis finished the study.

The field trials began in the spring of 1954. The results would not be known for one year. After getting their parents' approval, thousands of second graders lined up for vaccinations. Second-grade children were the most at risk for the disease. Salk

Dr. Salk vaccinates eight-year-old polio pioneer Gail Rosenthal as part of the field trials in Pittsburgh, Pennsylvania.

himself injected some of the youngsters. Ouch! These first children to be vaccinated became known as "polio pioneers."

Why would so many parents say yes to an injection they knew almost nothing about? Remember the fear that surrounded polio? That was enough to make most Americans willing to trust their children to this quiet, mild-mannered scientist who hoped he could stop the disease.

Thirty-three states took part in the polio vaccine field trials. The task was gigantic and very expensive. The trials cost about $7,500,000! Nearly one million children were studied. The first child to receive the vaccine was six-year-old Randy Kerr of McLean, Virginia. On the twenty-fifth anniversary of the field trials, in 1980, Randy Kerr and Jonas Salk met for the first time.

It was a long, hard year waiting for the results. But when they came—oh, what a glorious day! It was April 12, 1955, the tenth anniversary of the death of Franklin Roosevelt. Dr. Thomas Francis Jr., director of the Poliomyelitis Vaccine Evaluation Center at the University of Michigan, said four words. Francis declared, "Safe, effective, and potent." It had taken hundreds of years to make these four words real. By potent, Francis meant powerful. Polio, the killer disease, was about to be knocked right out of the ring.

The report said that the vaccine was 80 to 90 percent effective against two of the three types of poliovirus and 60 to 70 percent effective against the third type. Salk assured everyone that his new vaccine could be nearly 100 percent effective. This shocked the scientific community.

Jonas Salk was not bragging. In 1952, more than 57,000 Americans were reported to have

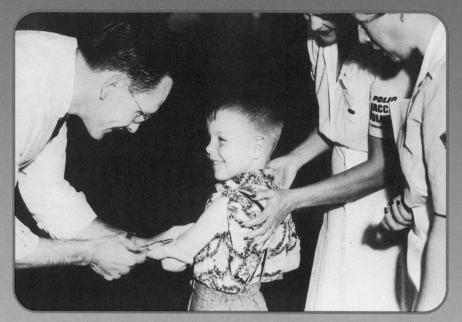

In an important historic moment, polio pioneer Randy Kerr receives the first polio vaccination of the field trials.

Jonas Salk (left) finally meets the first polio pioneer, Randy Kerr, in Washington, D.C., on April 11, 1980

poliomyelitis. In 1953 and 1954, the two years before the killed poliovirus vaccine began to be widely used, there were about 38,000 cases of poliomyelitis each summer. In 1957, after only three years of using the killed poliovirus vaccine, there were fewer than 6,000 cases of poliomyelitis, the lowest level since 1942. It took just one generation from that day in 1955 to erase polio from the memory of most Americans. Today, polio is just about gone. The World Health Organization (WHO) has predicted that polio will soon be gone from the entire world.

Dr. Jonas Salk became a hero overnight. Many thought he would win the Nobel Prize for medicine, but he did not. President Dwight D. Eisenhower invited the Salk family to the White House, and Salk received a Congressional Medal of Honor. He also received honorary degrees from several universities and thousands of letters from children all over the country. Schools were named after him, and lots of baby boys in the mid-1950s were named Jonas.

Salk never took money for his vaccine. When asked who owned it, he replied, "Well, the people, I would say. There is no patent. Could you patent the sun?" Although Salk meant that the vaccine belonged to everyone, just as the sun belongs to

The announcement of the successful polio vaccine was all over the newspaper headlines.

everyone, some of the other scientists didn't like the remark. They thought he was bragging, once again taking all the credit for the vaccine instead of crediting the work that had gone on before him.

When Salk believed he was right, he was not bothered much by criticism. He went about his life and his work as usual. Indeed, perhaps, part of his success was the need to solve a problem in his own way. These qualities of focus and ambition may have made fellow scientists dislike Salk, but they are also partly responsible for his success.

The criticism may not have bothered Jonas Salk, but being famous did. He wanted to be left alone to be a research scientist. So, he decided to leave the University of Pittsburgh. The most famous man of

Eager mothers awaiting the first polio vaccinations line up with their children outside a clinic.

the time could have done many things. What he did, in 1963, was get financial aid from the National Foundation and a gift of land from San Diego, California. He opened the Salk Institute of Biological Studies in nearby La Jolla. Again, Salk was looking for a new medical challenge.

By the time Salk opened his institute, strangely enough, the vaccine that made him world famous was going out of use. Like Salk, Dr. Sabin had never given up. But now it looked like Salk's old rival was successful. Sabin's live virus vaccine had proved effective and it was thought to have two advantages over Salk's killed virus vaccine. The protection might last longer, and it was given as liquid drops in the mouth. No more needles, no more "ouches" in the medical office. Little by little, Salk's great discovery was replaced by the easier to use, supposedly more effective vaccine of Dr. Albert Sabin.

Sabin, of course, was very pleased. Salk obviously was not, but he did not comment much except to discuss fears of possible problems with giving a live virus vaccine. These men were both dedicated scientists, but they were also real rivals in the world of scientific research.

Sabin died in 1993, still upset about Salk's success. He said of Salk's vaccine, "It was pure kitchen chemistry. Salk didn't discover anything."

But Salk now had turned his full attention to his new institute. He was busier than ever. There are just so many hours in a day and days in a week. And just so many places to be. Something had to give. Salk's marriage ended. After twenty-nine years, the

Salks divorced in 1968. Two years later, Jonas Salk married Françoise Gilot, an artist from France.

His son, Peter Salk, talked about how he and his brothers felt about growing up with a famous father who was dedicated to his work. "He was rarely home, so he didn't spend time playing catch and games like the other fathers. But in the summers there would be more time together, for swimming, sailing, or water skiing. Even then, Dad would spend much of his time on his work. I remember the time in the early 1950s on Lake Erie, where we rented a cottage for seven summers. There were about fifteen or twenty cottages in the area but only one telephone. It was hung on a pole. Whenever it rang, anyone nearby would answer it. But since the calls were mostly for Dad, he finally installed our own phone, the first private one in the cottage colony."

Although Salk never insisted that his sons become doctors, they all went to medical school. Says Peter, "It's like the wake of a boat. He was such a powerful figure that he swept us along without actually trying."

From the time Salk's institute opened until 1984, he kept his own lab there. Then seventy years old, he thought it might be time to retire, perhaps to do

Jonas Salk with his second wife, Françoise Gilot

some writing. But instead, he began working on a new threat—AIDS, or acquired immune deficiency syndrome.

AIDS is a deadly disease that attacks and destroys the human immune system. There is no cure and no vaccine. Salk saw AIDS as a line of research that was not being followed in the correct way. If it were to be done correctly, he'd have to do it himself. This was the quiet arrogance that annoyed his colleagues. But remember that Salk once said, "Life is not a popularity contest."

Until his death of heart failure on June 23, 1995, at the age of eighty, Jonas Salk moved ahead with his work in his own way. In the late 1980s, he did develop an experimental vaccine treatment for AIDS and at his death was working on plans for its trial. Obviously Peter Salk was right when he said of his famous father, "Until he died, he didn't let go."

In 1999, the work of Salk and Sabin was once again front-page news. In 1979, the last outbreak of polio was reported in the United States—ten cases. But in 1997, there were five cases of polio that developed from the vaccine. Throughout the 1990s, about eight cases a year were recorded.

The Centers for Disease Control and Prevention decided to switch vaccines again. As of January 1, 2000, the Sabin vaccine is rarely used in the United States. U.S. children are once again injected with the killed virus vaccine developed by Salk. The ouch is back.

The Sabin vaccine is still used in some countries where health care facilities are poor. In these poorer countries, an outbreak must be stopped immediately. Sabin's live virus is easier to give and therefore can be given more quickly to stop an epidemic.

Sabin's oral polio vaccine is given to children in India in a countrywide campaign in 1999 to end the spread of the disease.

The threat of polio is gone for almost all Americans and for the majority of people throughout the world. But for those who got polio before the vaccines were developed, there are still problems. In the 1980s, doctors began to notice that people who had polio thirty or forty years before were having trouble again. Even if they weren't originally paralyzed, they began to experience weakness in the limbs, along with other medical problems.

Known as PPS, or post polio syndrome, it is little understood. However, scientists think that nerve damage caused by the virus years ago is just now surfacing. With no cure yet, for these people it is like fighting polio all over again.

Perhaps if Jonas Salk had lived long enough, he would have tackled PPS. If not, there would have been other problems for his attention. He was a quiet man, a loner, brilliant and dedicated to his goals. His work, Salk once said, was an "assault on the unreasonableness of life."

To the thousands of young Americans in the mid-twentieth century, and all those since, he was the man who gave them freedom from fear. In 1993, he said, "Freedom from fear is the most powerful of all emotions. Franklin Roosevelt, who had polio, said, 'There is nothing to fear but fear itself.' I learned how important freeing people from fear can be."

Although a giant in his field, Salk never won the Nobel Prize or became a member of the National Academy of Sciences. Many scientists saw him as competitive, stubborn, and arrogant. He was often pushed away from the medical world of which he was a part, but he was also adored by those he helped. Through it all, he remained his own person, his eyes always on the next scientific mystery to be solved. "I've learned enough in my life," he said, "to know that I must go my own way." And so he did.

Dr. Jonas Salk believed in himself and continued his work until his death in 1995.

Indeed, Salk followed his own advice: "Rise above the problem and never let go until it's solved."

Jonas Salk was a confident man, above all a man who believed in himself and did not glory in praise. In its June 30, 1995, edition, shortly after his death and more than forty years after the first announcement of the polio vaccine, the *San Diego Union* printed a cartoon. It shows a young boy standing in front of Jonas Salk's tombstone. The boy wears a T-shirt that says "Future generations." In back of him, lying on the ground, are leg braces that are no longer needed. Says the boy, speaking for the world,

"Thank you, sir."

Chronology

1914   Jonas Salk is born in New York City on October 28.

1916   The polio epidemic hits the east coast of the United States.

1926   Salk enters Townsend Harris High School.

1929   Salk graduates high school and enters CCNY.

1934   Salk graduates CCNY and enters the New York University College of Medicine.

1939   Salk graduates from the New York University College of Medicine on June 8; he marries Donna Lindsay on June 9.

1940   Salk interns at Mount Sinai Hospital, New York City.

1943– Salk joins the lab of Dr. Thomas Francis Jr.
1951   in Michigan, and they work on the influenza vaccine. Then, Salk undertakes a three-year study on polio types, and he decides on the killed virus as a workable vaccine.

1952   In June, Salk's vaccine is tested on humans at the D.T. Watson Home for Crippled Children near Pittsburgh.

1953	The polio vaccine is announced to the public on March 26.
1954	Field trials begin on Salk's vaccine. The first children to be inoculated are known as polio pioneers.
1955	Field trials prove that Salk's vaccine works; the announcement is made on the tenth anniversary of the death of President Franklin D. Roosevelt, April 12.
1963	Salk Institute of Biological Studies opens in La Jolla, California.
1968	Salk and his wife get divorced.
1970	Salk marries Françoise Gilot.
1980	The twenty-fifth anniversary of the polio field trials. Salk finally meets Randy Kerr, the first child who received the vaccine.
1993	Dr. Albert Sabin dies.
1995	Jonas Salk dies on June 23.
1999	WHO declares polio will soon be eliminated from the world.

For More Information

BOOKS

Curson, Marjorie. *Jonas Salk*. Morristown, NJ: Silver-Burdett, 1990.

Salk, Jonas. *Survival of the Wisest*. New York: Harper, 1973.

Sherrow, Victoria. *Jonas Salk*. New York: Facts On File, 1993.

Tomlinson, Michael. *Jonas Salk*. Vero Beach, FL: The Rourke Book Company, 1993.

WEB SITES

Epidemic! On the Trail of Killer Diseases
http://www.discovery.com/exp/epidemic/polio/polio.html
This Web site displays the history of the polio epidemic
and the search for a vaccine.

The Hall of Science and Exploration
http://www.achievement.org/autodoc/page/sal0pro-1
A summary of Salk's contributions to science. Site includes a biography,
photographs, and an interview with Jonas Salk.

People and Discoveries: Jonas Salk 1914–1995
http://www.pbs.org/wgbh/aso/databank/entries/bmsalk.html
This Web site displays a brief biography of Jonas Salk.

Postpolio.org
http://www.postpolio.org/
This Web site explains post-polio syndrome and includes many relevant
links.

Index

Page numbers in italics
refer to illustrations.